MW00928640

How to prepare for the ascent of Mount Kilimanjaro?

Get ready for the adventure of a lifetime.

4

"To stay is to exist,
but to travel, is to live."

Gustave Nadaud

SUMMARY

Introduction   11

1. Introduction to Mount Kilimanjaro and its various
    hiking routes   15
2. Fitness assessment and training tips for the climb   33
3. Hiking equipment required   43
        Packing list   62
4. Psychological preparation and stress management
    for the climb   70
5. Choosing a reliable travel agency and calculating
    your budget   80
6. Preparing your hiking gear and organizing your
    backpack   103
7. Tips for acclimating to oxygen deprivation and
    altitude   110
8. Tips for dealing with health and safety issues during
    the climb   119
9. Tips for respecting the environment and Mount
    Kilimanjaro's ecosystem   123

Conclusion   129

A few words to know before starting your trip in Tanzania:

Jambo : hello
Pole pole : slowly
Asante sana : thank you very much
Karibu : you're welcome, but also welcome
Hapana asante : no thank you
Hakuna matata : no problem, no worries

Introduction

When I decided to take up the challenge of climbing Kilimanjaro, I had no idea of the physical and mental challenges it would entail. I'm not a great sportswoman, so climbing the 5,895 meters was a real challenge for me. Yet, I managed to reach the summit of Africa's highest mountain.

A few days of breathtaking panoramas. Every day was a gift from nature, with sunrises and sunsets each more beautiful than the last. I felt so small in the face of nature's immensity, but it gave me the strength to go all the way and discover more. Reaching the summit took me through every emotion: the pride of having accomplished it, the relief of having finally arrived, the love of having shared this moment with incredible people, the joy of feeling free... A few tears rolled down my cheeks and I said to myself, this is life. This is the happiness and freedom I'm looking for when I travel, and I'm happy to have found it.

In this booklet, I share all the tips and advice to help you prepare effectively for this expedition. From physical preparation to logistics to mental preparation tips, I'll give you all my tips and tricks. My personal story is here to show you that climbing Kilimanjaro is a challenge that can be taken up by anyone. The most important thing is to enjoy every moment of this unforgettable journey.

Bear in mind that these are only general suggestions and that you should find out more about each subject before setting off to climb Mount Kilimanjaro.

Enjoy your reading!

1. Introduction to Mount Kilimanjaro and its various hiking routes

Mount Kilimanjaro is the highest mountain in Africa and is located in Tanzania. There are several hiking routes to the summit, each with its own advantages and disadvantages. It's important to choose the route that suits you best, based on your physical condition, hiking experience and budget.

Kilimanjaro

Climbing Mount Kilimanjaro is an incredible adventure waiting to happen! It's one of the most famous mountains in the world, and for good reason: it's the highest mountain in Africa, culminating at 5,895 meters above sea level. It is located in Tanzania, near the border between Kenya and Tanzania, and attracts thousands of climbers and hikers from all over the world every year.

Kilimanjaro is made up of three volcanoes: Kibo, Mawenzi and Shira. The highest peak, Uhuru Peak, is located on the Kibo volcano. Its ascent is accessible to all levels of fitness and hiking experience, but it's important to prepare well and plan your route carefully. There are several routes to the summit, each with its own advantages and disadvantages. We'll look at these a little later in this booklet.

One of the major challenges of climbing Mount Kilimanjaro is acclimatization to the altitude and the lower oxygen levels. To help your body adapt, take your time and adopt a slow, steady pace. Something you'll often hear from your guide is **"Pole Pole"**, which means "slowly" in Swahili. So avoid intense efforts for the first few days, and don't hesitate to drink plenty of water and eat carbohydrate-rich foods to help your body adapt.

As it is forbidden to climb the mountain without a guide, it is strongly recommended that you use an experienced travel agency for this ascent. These agencies will help you plan your steps and work with qualified guides who will advise you on acclimatization, health and safety during the climb. Agencies can usually lend you certain equipment you don't want to buy yourself (poles, gloves, jacket, etc.).

Mount Kilimanjaro is considered one of the most difficult mountains to climb in terms of altitude acclimatization, because as well as being the highest mountain in Africa, Kilimanjaro is the highest free-standing mountain in the world. The fact that it is free-standing means that no other mountain touches it, which makes the challenges of climbing it all the more difficult. For example, the climate is unpredictable and can change rapidly, with snowstorms and strong winds. Also, its high altitude often causes headaches and nausea. And finally, there's little oxygen available at this altitude, making breathing more difficult. But don't worry, if you're well accompanied and prepared both physically and mentally, you'll be able to overcome the challenges of altitude, cold and hostile environment to reach the summit of this magnificent mountain. It requires no mountaineering skills and is therefore accessible to all.

Finally, climbing Mount Kilimanjaro can be stressful for most of us, especially if, like me, it's your first time. So it's important to prepare yourself mentally and manage your stress before you set off. Find out what you can expect during the climb. To do this, I recommend watching YouTube videos filmed and published by hikers like you and me, who share their adventure with us. Personally, these videos really moved me and motivated me to reach the summit myself!

As an aside, did you know that to date (2023), the youngest person to have climbed Kilimanjaro was 7 and the oldest 89? Kilimanjaro is not only a unique experience, it's also accessible to everyone, whatever your age! So take the plunge and experience unforgettable moments.

The routes

If you already have an idea of which route you're going to choose, or if you're still unsure, I'd be delighted to help you make your decision. However, it's important to understand that we're all different, and it's essential to study the different options carefully before choosing the one that's right for YOU.

To reach the summit of Mount Kilimanjaro, there are several hiking routes, each with its own pros and cons. It's important to choose the route that suits you best, based on your physical condition, hiking experience and budget.
Here are some examples of popular routes, but please note that walking times and camp locations may vary according to the travel agency and guide chosen.

Having personally done the Lemosho route over seven days, I'd recommend it to hikers looking for a rustic route through a variety of beautiful landscapes with plenty of time to acclimatize. Physically, I didn't find the days impossible to complete, and I loved the change of scenery along the way. Every day was a feast for the eyes. I got to see Kilimanjaro from different angles, and it's simply breathtaking!

On the following page, you'll find a map of the various routes.

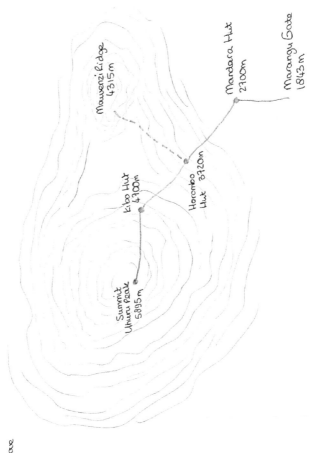

Marangu
Route

View from above

Rongai
Route

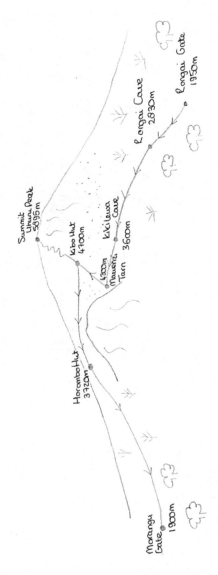

Summit
Uhuru Peak
5895m

Kibo Hut
4700m

Kikelewa Cave

4330m
Mawenzi
Tarn

3600m

Rongai Cave
2830m

Rongai Gate
1950m

Horombo Hut
3720m

Marangu
Gate
1900m

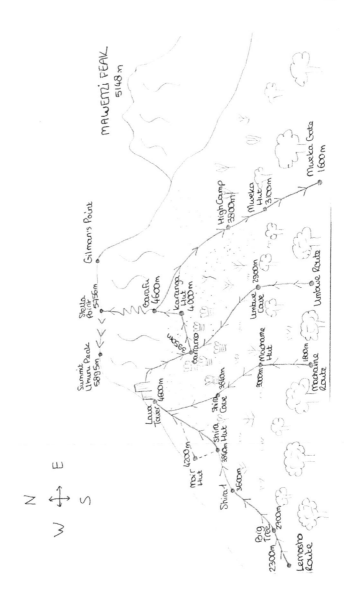

Here are the most popular routes in more detail:

Marangu Route :

The Marangu Route is considered the easiest, as it is relatively well developed and offers easy access to waterholes. It can be completed in five or six days and is known for its huts with beds and showers, making it more comfortable than other routes. However, it is also the busiest and can be crowded during the high season.

This route is also considered the least interesting in terms of hiking, as it doesn't offer views as spectacular as the others, and the descent is via the same road as the ascent.

The Marangu Route is recommended for those in good physical condition, but who are looking for a relatively easy, short-distance route to the summit of Mount Kilimanjaro. However, it's important to remember that climbing Kilimanjaro is a demanding physical challenge and even the easiest route can be difficult for some people. Much depends on your body and how it adapts to the altitude. It's still an intense route, as it takes five to six days to complete, which is relatively short for altitude acclimatization.

Day 1: The Marangu Route starts at Marangu Gate, at an altitude of 1,843 meters. You'll hike for around five hours to reach the first Mandara Hut, at 2,700 meters above sea level.

Day 2: You'll hike for around six to seven hours to reach the second shelter Horombo Hut, located at an altitude of 3,720 meters.

Day 3: Three to four hours round trip to Mawenzi Ridge (4,315 m) to acclimatize. This stage can be omitted if you decide to do the route in 5 days.

Day 4: Afterwards, you'll hike for around six to eight hours to reach the Kibo Hut refuge, situated at an altitude of 4,700 meters.

Day 5: The most intense day, as you'll hike for around seven hours to reach Uhuru Peak, at 5,895 meters above sea level. You will then descend for around four hours to Horombo Hut, where you will spend the night.

Day 6: You'll spend around six hours descending to the start gate and complete your ascent.

If you're looking for a relatively easy and, above all, comfortable route, this is the one for you.

Machame Route :

The Machame Route is the most popular route. It takes six or seven days to complete and offers superb views of the surrounding area. The Machame Route is known to be a little more difficult than the Marangu Route, but it is less crowded and offers more varied scenery. Nights are spent in tents.

Here's how the ascent via the Machame Route usually goes:

Day 1: You'll start your ascent at Machame Gate, at an altitude of 1,640 meters. You'll hike for around six hours to reach Machame Camp, at 2,850 meters above sea level, where you'll spend the night.

Day 2: You'll hike for around six hours to reach the second camp, called Shira 2 Camp, at an altitude of 3,810 meters.

Day 3: You'll hike for around five hours to reach Lava Tower camp at 4,630 meters altitude, where you'll stay a short while to acclimatize. You'll then continue with a three-hour hike to Barranco Camp, at 3,970 meters above sea level.

Day 4: You'll hike for around five hours to reach Karanga Camp, situated at an altitude of 3,995 meters.

Day 5: You'll hike for around three hours to reach Barafu Camp, situated at an altitude of 4,670 meters.

Day 6: The most intense day, as you hike for around seven to eight hours to reach Uhuru Peak, at 5,895 metres above sea level. Then you'll descend for around four to six hours to Mweka Camp at 3,100 meters altitude, where you'll spend the night.

Day 7: You'll descend for three to four hours to Mweka Gate and complete your ascent.

If you want to do this route in six days instead of seven, days four and five will be combined and you won't spend the night at Karanga Camp.

Umbwe Route :

The Umbwe Route is one of the least-frequented and most challenging routes, due to the rapid climb in altitude to the summit of Mount Kilimanjaro. It takes six to seven days to complete and is recommended for experienced hikers. The Umbwe Route is renowned for its breathtaking views of the surrounding area, and with lower visitor numbers than the other routes, it is also more rustic. Nights are spent in tents.

Day 1: The route starts at Umbwe Gate, situated at an altitude of 1,600 meters. On the first day, you'll hike for around six to seven hours to reach Umbwe Camp, at an altitude of 2,940 meters.

Day 2: You'll hike for around five hours to reach Barranco Camp, situated at an altitude of 3,970 meters.

Day 3: You will hike for around five hours to reach Karanga Camp, situated at an altitude of 3,995 meters.

Day 4: You will hike for around five hours to reach Barafu Camp, at an altitude of 4,600 meters.

Day 5: The most intense day, as you'll hike for around seven to eight hours to reach Uhuru Peak, at 5,895 meters above sea level. Then you'll descend for around four to six hours to Mweka Camp at 3,100 meters altitude, where you'll spend the night.

Day 6: You'll descend for three to four hours to Mweka Gate and complete your ascent.

The seven-day variant adds an acclimatization day between the second and third day at Barranco camp.
The Umbwe Route is recommended for experienced hikers looking for a more challenging, less crowded route.

Rongai Route :

The Rongai Route is also one of the less-frequented routes and the only one that approaches Kilimanjaro from the north. It takes six to seven days to complete and offers beautiful views of the surrounding area. Being less crowded than other routes, it offers a more authentic hiking experience. Nights arc spent in tents.

Day 1: This route begins at Rongai Gate, situated at an altitude of 1,950 meters. Then you'll hikc for around four hours to reach the first Rongai Cave camp, at 2,830 meters above sea level.

Day 2: You'll hike for around four hours to reach Second Cave camp, at an altitude of 3,450 meters. You then continue for another four hours to Kikelewa Cave at 3,600 meters above sea level.

Day 3: You will be walking for around four hours to reach the Mawenzi Tarn camp, situated at an altitude of 4,300 meters.

Day 4: Three to four hours round trip to Mawenzi Ridge (4,315 m) to acclimatize. This stage can be omitted if you decide to do the route in six days.

Day 5: You'll hike for around six hours to reach Kibo Hut, situated at an altitude of 4,700 meters.

Day 6: The most intense day, as you'll hike for around seven hours to reach Uhuru Peak, at 5,895 meters above sea level. Then you'll descend for around four hours on the other side of the mountain to Horombo Hut, at 3,720 meters, where you'll spend the night.

Day 7: Descend for five to seven hours to Marangu Gate, where you complete your ascent.

If you're looking for a less crowded, more rustic route, the Rongai Route is for you!

Lemosho Route (the one I chose) :

The Lemosho Route is considered Kilimanjaro's most scenic itinerary, offering panoramic views of the mountain's various slopes. It takes seven to eight days to complete, and nights are spent in tents. The route is little used until it joins the Machame Route near Lava Tower.

Day 1: The route starts at Lemosho Gate, at an altitude of 2,100 meters. You'll hike for about three hours to reach the first camp, Mti Mkubwa, at 2,650 meters above sea level.

Day 2: You'll hike for around eight to ten hours to reach Shira II Camp, situated at an altitude of 3,850 meters.

Day 3: You'll hike for around five to six hours to reach Lava Tower camp, situated at 4,630 meters above sea level, where you'll stay for a short time to acclimatize. You'll then continue with a three-hour hike to Barranco Camp, at an altitude of 3,970 meters.

Day 4: You will walk for around five hours to reach Karanga Camp, at an altitude of 3,995 meters.

Day 5: You will hike for around three hours to reach Barafu Camp, at an altitude of 4,600 meters.

Day 6: The most intense day, as you hike for around seven to eight hours to reach Uhuru Peak, at 5,895 meters above sea level. You will then descend for around four to six hours to Mweka Camp at 3,100 meters altitude, where you will spend the night.

Day 7: Descend for three to four hours to Mweka Gate and complete your ascent.

Whatever path you choose, anyone can succeed! However, it's important to prepare carefully, but believe me, it's worth it! In addition to the physical challenges, you may also face difficulties acclimatizing to the lack of oxygen and the altitude, but your guide will always be close to give you the right advice. Personally, when I took the Lemosho route over seven days, I didn't experience any major altitude-related difficulties. I only suffered a slight headache on the fourth and fifth day, which could be treated with some medication. In my opinion, the most difficult walking days were day two, because of its long duration (around 8h30), and day six, which corresponds to the ascent to the summit. It was very steep and difficult. During the 6-hour 45-minute climb, I experienced altitude-related symptoms such as dizziness and stomach cramps. The sixth day is also very long, because once you've reached the summit, you immediately have to start the descent, which can take up to six hours of walking.

IMPORTANT: When choosing your itinerary, bear in mind that the longer the route, the more time you'll have to acclimatize, which will reduce the risk of developing symptoms of mountain sickness and increase your chances of reaching the summit.

2. Fitness assessment and training tips for the climb

Now that you know the different routes, one of the first steps is to make sure you're physically ready for the adventure. Climbing Kilimanjaro is physical, with some days lasting around ten hours, so it's important to prepare yourself to avoid injury and increase your chances of success.

The first step in assessing your physical condition is to consult your doctor. Make sure you're in good shape, and that you don't have any health problems that could pose a problem during the climb (blood pressure problems, for example, can be dangerous at altitude). For a second opinion, you can consult a doctor specializing in mountain medicine, who will inform you if you have any contraindications to this activity and especially to this altitude. This is not mandatory, and personally I haven't done it, but if you have any doubts about your health, do it. Climbing Kilimanjaro involves risks of altitude sickness, which can be serious or fatal if not taken into account, so it's best to get professional advice to avoid taking any unnecessary risks. Don't worry, I'm warning you about a lot of things, but you're not climbing Mount Everest either! The aim here is to understand that there may be a risk, and to consult a professional so that you can set off with peace of mind.

Your doctor will also advise you on what medicines and what precautions to take. Depending on your country of origin, Tanzania may require certain vaccinations. Normally, if you are traveling from Europe, no vaccinations are required. If you're afraid of altitude, he may prescribe medication for this.

Next, I advise you to determine your current level of physical activity using a simple scale such as "inactive", "slightly active", "moderately active" or "very active". If you are inactive or slightly active, it's important to follow a balanced, progressive training program that targets strength and endurance, and to increase your level of physical activity gradually.

Muscle strengthening

A multitude of exercises can help strengthen your body for the Kilimanjaro climb. Here are a few that are particularly effective in strengthening the muscles most in demand during the climb.

To strengthen the legs:
- **<u>Squats</u>** strengthen the quadriceps, hamstrings and glutes.

- **<u>Lunges</u>** strengthen the quadriceps, hamstrings and inner and outer thigh muscles.
- **<u>Calf raises</u>** strengthen the calves and were particularly helpful on the last day, when I reached the summit after almost 7 hours walking on a steep slope.

To strengthen the torso and shoulders:
- **<u>Push-ups</u>** strengthen pectorals, triceps and shoulders.
- **<u>Pull-ups</u>** strengthen the back and biceps.
- **<u>Deadlifts</u>** can strengthen shoulders, arms and back.

Of course, not everyone is at the same level, and not everyone has access to all the necessary equipment. So I advise you to make do with what you've got. For example, if you want to do weight lifting, replace the weights with water bottles. Or if you can't do full push-ups, do them on your knees. Many alternative exercises to do at home are available on the Internet.

To strengthen the core:
- **<u>Abdominals</u>**
- **<u>Spinal stretching</u>**
- **<u>Front and side crunches</u>** in several series of 30-second crunches followed by 30-second rests.

These exercises strengthen the core muscles.

Endurance

There are several activities that can help improve your
stamina for the Kilimanjaro climb:

- **Walking or running** on hilly terrain and mountain
  trails: this will help you get used to walking on
  sloping ground and increase your cardiovascular
  endurance.

- **Mountain biking** : this will strengthen your legs and
  help you get used to inclined terrain and steep
  slopes.

- **Swimming** : This activity mainly involves the
  muscles of the arms, shoulders, legs and back, while
  improving breathing and blood circulation. By
  swimming regularly, you increase your
  cardiovascular capacity, i.e. your ability to supply
  oxygen to your muscles during prolonged physical
  activity.

- **Hiking with a backpack** : porters will carry 90% of
  your belongings, but remember that you'll still be
  carrying a small backpack, in which you'll carry
  what you need for the day (2 to 3L of water, jacket,
  gloves, hat, medication, snacks, etc.). You'll need to
  get used to walking with a load on your back.

- **Other cardiovascular endurance workouts** :
exercise bike or elliptical trainer. The exercise bike
works leg muscles, which can help strengthen thighs
and calves. The elliptical is similar to the exercise
bike, but it also works the muscles of the arms and
shoulders.

The idea of these workouts is to accustom your body to
producing a long effort, so don't try to be at your best for 15
minutes. On the contrary, I advise you to favor long, low-
intensity outings.

Resistance

To improve your stamina, here are a few activities that are
particularly effective (depending on your personal abilities).

- **Circuit training** : this will help you strengthen your
whole body by alternating cardio and strength
training exercises.

- **High-intensity interval training (HIIT)** : this will
increase your cardiovascular and muscular stamina
by alternating periods of intense effort and recovery.
Start with low-intensity workouts and gradually
increase the intensity. You can easily find free
workouts on YouTube.

- **<u>Training with free weights, dumbbells or elastic bands</u>** : this will strengthen your muscles and increase your muscular resistance. Start with light weights and gradually increase the load.

If you're not used to exercising regularly, it's strongly recommended that you start training at least four months before you leave. Establish a progressive training rhythm, gradually increasing intensity, load and frequency. Don't forget to rest well between each training session, stay hydrated to avoid injury. To avoid monotony and stimulate different muscle groups, try to vary your activities. All training will be useful throughout the climb, whether it's for the ascent or the descent.

To get organized, I advise you to draw up a schedule that takes into account your private and professional life. We all have different schedules and workloads, so the number and duration of workouts will depend on you and your free time. To give you an idea, my schedule was made up as follows:
- One or two cardio/running sessions per week (endurance)
- One or two muscle-strengthening/HIIT sessions per week (strengthening and resistance)
- A long hiking trip over the weekend (endurance, strengthening and resistance).

And if possible, train in the mountains. This will get you used to the oxygen depletion and physical effort associated with altitude. But don't worry if this isn't possible: low-altitude training is obviously effective. It's important to adapt to your environment and progress at your own pace. Even though my personal training took place at low altitude, far from Kilimanjaro's 5,895 meters, I was able to progress at my own pace and be ready for the climb.

As with all sports training, nutrition is a crucial part of preparation. A balanced diet rich in essential nutrients is necessary to provide your body with the energy and nutrients it needs to function efficiently. Remember to eat enough protein, carbohydrates and healthy fats to maintain energy levels and repair damaged muscle tissue.

Throughout the climb, a chef will be on hand to prepare balanced meals that will give you enough strength for your days of walking. Their menus have been carefully designed to ensure that the food is easy to digest and provides enough energy. Expect fresh vegetables, fruit, meat and snacks along the way, as well as clean, purified water. If you have any special requests regarding your menu, don't worry, they accommodate all dietary needs (vegetarian or vegan, for example) and allergies.

Here's what you can expect for each meal:
- Breakfast: tea/coffee/hot chocolate, toast, jam/peanut butter/honey, eggs/sausages, porridge/pancakes, fresh fruit.
- Lunch: tea/coffee/hot chocolate, soup, pasta with beef sauce, vegetables, fresh fruit.
- Snacks: tea/coffee/hot chocolate, local cookies and popcorn.
- Dinner: tea/coffee/hot chocolate, soup, rice with chicken and vegetable sauce, avocado salad, fresh fruit.

Believe me, you won't starve! Meals are really a good convivial moment, and I have excellent memories of them.
In addition to food, whether you're training or climbing, make sure you're well hydrated to avoid dehydration and headaches.

In summary, to prepare yourself physically for climbing Mount Kilimanjaro, I recommend following a balanced training program that targets strength, endurance and stamina. For greater effectiveness, combine these activities with altitude training, backpack training, a balanced diet and good hydration. It's important to only do exercises that you feel comfortable with and that you can do around your home. By doing exercises that suit you, you'll be more motivated to continue training regularly and progressively without injuring yourself. Start slowly, but above all, be regular.

By following these tips, you'll be able to rise to the physical challenge of climbing Kilimanjaro and enjoy this incredible experience with complete pcacc of mind!

3. Hiking equipment required

Hiking equipment is an essential element not to be neglected. With unstable weather conditions in the mountains, you need to choose high-quality, comfortable and reliable equipment.

The shoes

First of all, hiking boots are the most important part of your equipment. You need to choose shoes that are comfortable, stable and offer good support for your feet and ankles. Hiking boots with high uppers are generally the most suitable for climbing Kilimanjaro, as they offer good support for the ankles and protection from rocks and stones. I advise you to choose shoes that are waterproof but also breathable, to avoid wet feet and blisters. It's a good idea to test them out before setting off for a minimum distance of 100 kilometers, to avoid pain or blisters during the climb.

Choose shoes that are at least 1 size larger, so that you don't touch the toe on descents, and so that you can wear them with thick socks, as the altitude will make your feet cold. Make sure you're not too cramped to avoid blisters and to maintain good walking comfort even with thicker socks.

There are many brands of quality hiking boots on the market, each with its own advantages. Here are a few popular and well-known brands:

- Salomon: a Swiss brand offering a wide range of hiking boots for all levels and types of terrain. Salomon shoes are renowned for their quality, comfort and durability.

- Salewa: a German brand renowned for its hiking boots designed to offer good support for feet and ankles, grip on difficult terrain and water resistance. They are also designed to be comfortable and adaptable to all types of terrain.

- La Sportiva: an Italian brand renowned for its high-performance hiking boots, suitable for experienced hikers. These shoes are renowned for their quality, performance on difficult terrain and water resistance.

- Lowa: a German brand with a range of hiking boots for experienced hikers. They are renowned for their quality, comfort and water resistance.

- Merrell: an American brand offering quality hiking boots for hikers of all levels. Merrell shoes are renowned for their comfort, grip and water resistance.

Personally, I bought the Rapace GTX model from Salewa and I don't regret my choice. Very comfortable on the feet, they breathe, resist water and offer good stability when walking thanks to the good grip of the crampons. The same model is also available for men, tested and approved by my partner!

A little tip : take a comfortable pair of shoes with you that you can wear in the evening after your day's walking. Following a friend's advice, I brought Crocs with thick socks and it was the best thing I ever did. At the end of our long days of walking, my feet thanked me!

The backpack

Another very important piece of equipment is the backpack, because you need to choose one that's comfortable to wear, has good back support and has enough room for all your gear. I'd like to make it clear that this is the bag you'll be carrying yourself on the day's hike, with only your essentials. Hiking backpacks between 30 and 45 liters are generally the most suitable for this type of ascent, as they offer enough space for all the gear you'll need during the day and are small enough to remain comfortable on mountain trails. It's also important to check that it has enough pockets to store your belongings and straps to secure equipment outside the bacpack, such as your walking poles.

Specialized hiking backpacks usually come with a removable rain cape that you can put over your bag in case of rain. If you don't have one, consider buying one separately.

When selecting your bag, also bear in mind that you'll need to carry a 2 to 3L water pouch, so choose one with a dedicated compartment and hose outlet. This will make it easier to organize your bag.

Here are a few well-known brands that I personally appreciate for their quality hiking bags:
- Deuter
- Millet
- Osprey
- Lowe Alpine.

After a careful analysis of the various models available on the market, I opted for the Millet Ubic 40 (40L) backpack for its comfort, sturdiness and the presence of a sufficient number of inside and outside pockets. This unisex model also satisfied my partner, who also used it during the climb.

In addition to all these criteria, make sure the backpack is adapted to your morphology and that you know how to adjust it so that it's comfortable to wear.

The duffle bag

This is the bag that will be carried by the porters. Generally speaking, a 65 to 100-liter bag is recommended, as everything you don't carry with you during the day will have to fit in this bag. The number of kilos will be limited to between 10 and 14 kilos, so that the porter does not exceed the maximum weight authorized to be carried.

Duffle bags are generally made in elongated shapes and with robust, water-resistant materials, making them suitable for the variable weather conditions encountered on Kilimanjaro.

Here are the brands renowned for their quality, water-resistant duffle bags:
- The North Face
- Patagonia
- Forclaz
- And others.

I myself had opted for a 90L Tribord Adventure bag available from Decathlon. It's waterproof, very durable and has numerous compartments that helped me organize my belongings.

As explained, this bag will be carried by the porters who will accompany you on the climb. I'd like to make it clear that, when making your selection, you don't need to take into account the comfort of the bag on your back, as the porters will generally put it on their heads.

Containers to transport your water

To carry enough water for your day's walking, we recommend you take a water bag that can hold up to 3 liters. The higher you climb, the more important it becomes to drink. Firstly, because altitude can cause dehydration more quickly, as the air is drier and colder. This can lead to symptoms such as headaches, fatigue and reduced physical performance.

What's more, when you exercise in the mountains, your body works harder to maintain body temperature and fuel your muscles. This leads to increased sweating, and therefore additional water loss. So it's important to drink enough water to compensate for these losses and maintain a good level of hydration.

I advise you to drink your water in small sips throughout the day, rather than large gulps, to better assimilate it rather than evacuate it. Your guide will also be there to remind you of this, and will regularly tell you to "sippy sippy", which means to take small sips.

In addition to your water bag, your travel agent will also ask you to bring a one-liter water bottle that will only be used on the day of the summit climb. They'll fill this bottle with hot (or even boiling) water, so you'll have something to drink should the water in your pocket freeze in the sub-zero temperature at the summit.

For information, depending on the time of the year, the temperature at the summit is around -15 to -20 degrees and it's very windy.

Clothes

It is important to dress with consideration for the changing weather conditions you will encounter when climbing Mount Kilimanjaro. You should pack warm clothes for cold nights and rain gear for rainy days. Sounds logical right! It is also important to wear several small layers instead of one large layer, as this will allow you to remove them little by little depending on the temperature and physical effort. At first, you will quickly get hot if you have sun, but the weather can also change very quickly.

Well covered, I never felt cold at night, except maybe the last day. Being very cold, I was afraid of that, but rest assured, it is not too extreme except on the last day (during the climb to the summit).

Here is a list of clothes you should pack for climbing Kilimanjaro:

Internal layers

Sports underwear: light and comfortable sports underwear in breathable material to wick away perspiration.

Wool or synthetic base layers to keep you warm (no cotton). Consider leggings and long-sleeved cardigans or sweaters.

Upper mid-layer (like a fleece): A jacket or sweater that keeps you warm and that you can put on top of the base layer. You can find them at Cimalp, Patagonia or Columbia for example.

"Double skin" socks: these are socks that have two layers. This technique greatly reduces the risk of blisters. The friction is between the two socks and not on the foot. You can find some on the website of the French brand Cimalp. It was the first time I wore this type of socks and I was really satisfied.

Warm hiking socks: the higher you go, the colder it will be, so also remember to bring warmer socks.

Outer layers

Down jacket: the higher you go, the more the temperature drops. This is why the down jacket will be very useful during the climb to the summit where it will be very cold, but also for the evenings at camp. Choose a down jacket that is light to wear, breathable and warm. There are many brands that offer adequate down jackets, but it is still important to carefully check the characteristics to make the choice that meets your needs. Having no use for this type of jacket in my daily life, I decided to rent one from my travel agency.

Waterproof jacket (with a hood, of course): if you choose a quality jacket, it will protect you not only from the rain, but also from the wind. Personally, I opted for the Dryzzle FutureLight jacket from The North Face brand. It was great, I highly recommend it!

Hiking pants: These should allow you to feel comfortable lifting your legs when you have to climb over rocks and take long walks. For those who tend to get hot quickly, it may be a good idea to bring shorts for the first few days of hiking.

For information, the first 2 days of the trek, you will be hot (about 20 degrees). Then little by little the temperature will drop.

Rain pants: which you can put over your hiking pants. So remember to take a size or two above your usual size.

Headlamp

A headlamp is essential equipment for any multi-day hike. It will be useful not only during the night of the ascent to the summit, but also for the evening in your tent, for reading or going to the toilet. Choose a powerful headlamp that will sufficiently light your path during the night ascent, don't take the first price!

The most popular brands used by athletes for this type of activity are Petzl and Stoots, but there are also other options on the market.

Other equipment

There is other important equipment to think about such as gloves and liners, a hat, a cap, sunglasses (polarized if you have sensitive eyes), walking poles, a camera, an external battery (possibly rechargeable in the sun), a sports watch, a small towel, etc.

You can inquire with the agency you have selected to do the climb, but generally all reliable agencies provide the following equipment:

- High-quality, four-season mountain tents, accommodating two people each.
- Private toilets and a dedicated dining tent, reserved for climbers.
- Four-season sleeping bags that can withstand an environment generally of -18° C. And sleeping bag liners.
- Insulated sleeping mats.

Usually, agencies also offer certain equipment for rental. So if there are things that you prefer to rent instead of buying because you will not really need them after this climb, you can indicate this when booking.

In addition to this equipment, it is advisable to take a first aid kit containing bandages, mosquito repellent, tablets against malaria, basic medicines such as painkillers for headaches, as well as medicines for stomach aches, vomiting and diarrhea. During our ascent, we came across people who had brought altitude sickness medication. Although our group did not need them, it can be reassuring to have them with you. If you are interested in this type of medication, talk to your doctor.

Then, also remember to take sunscreen (with a high SPF against UVA and UVB), lip balm (with a high SPF), moisturizer (for face and hands) as well as hygienic products (altitude can disrupt your menstrual cycle - better be prepared ladies!).

Little tip: Bring snacks, your guilty pleasure, sweet like chocolate or cookies, or even salty like pistachios or peanuts. Believe me it will boost you and give you more positive energy which is crucial to reaching the top. Personally, I had brought Werther's candies in sweet and Doritos Bits in salty. After experience, I should have taken more salty snacks, first because I love it! but also because the Kilimanjaro team already gave us sweet snacks such as ginger cookies and chocolate.

Travel documents

There are several important documents to prepare before leaving for the ascent of Kilimanjaro. Here is the list of those you will need:

Valid passport: Make sure your passport is valid for the duration of your trip and has enough blank pages for visas and entry/exit stamps.

Visa : Be sure to check the visa requirements for entering Tanzania. In most cases, a single entry visa is required but check the requirements based on your nationality. You have the possibility to get a visa at the airport on arrival, but due to long queues, I encourage you to buy it online on : https://visa.immigration.go.tz/.

Plane ticket : Make sure you have confirmed air tickets for your round trip and flight information.

Vaccination certificate : It is recommended to get vaccinated against diseases like yellow fever, typhoid and meningitis when traveling to Tanzania. It is important to check with your doctor or a vaccination center about the vaccination requirements depending on your place of residence.

Travel insurance : It is mandatory to have travel insurance which covers accidents, illnesses, medical repatriations and cancellations. Your insurance policy should cover you for "hikes up to 6,000 m above sea level". I recommend True Traveller, they have a pack including Kilimanjaro.

Payment method : A credit card or dollars in cash. The local currency is the Tanzanian shilling, but the dollar is accepted almost everywhere in the country.

To conclude, this trip requires careful preparation and the choice of your hiking equipment is crucial to guarantee a safe and comfortable ascent. To help you prepare for your trip to Tanzania, you will find in the following section a detailed list of all the necessary equipment. This checklist will help you ensure that you don't forget anything and that you are ready to take on the challenge of this exceptional adventure.

Packing list for a 7 day trek

Making a detailed travel list, also called a packing list, is a crucial step in preparing for a trip. This step is even more important when it comes to a trip like climbing Kilimanjaro, because once you're on the mountain, it will be impossible for you to buy what you need. Having a packing list will help you avoid forgetting anything important that could negatively impact your trip and will ensure a successful and safe climb of Kilimanjaro.

I would like to point out that this packing list is based on my personal experience, that is to say an ascent over seven days. Certain quantities must be adapted depending on the number of days of your climb, I am thinking in particular of the number of t-shirts/undershirts, underwear and socks.

I also remind you that most of the time, your travel agency provides a certain number of equipment including:
-   High-quality, four-season mountain tents that can accommodate two people each.
-   Private toilets and a dedicated dining tent, reserved for climbers.

- Four-season sleeping bags that can withstand an environment generally of -18° C. And sleeping bag liners.
- Insulated sleeping mats.

It is important to validate this with them and modify the packing list accordingly.

You will find the packing list on the next page.

PACKING LIST

CARRYING EQUIPMENT

- Backpack with a capacity of 30 to 45L

- Backpack rain cover

- Waterproof duffle bag of 65 to 100L

- Reuseable, waterproof bags for equipment and clothes inside your duffel bag

- A water carrier (ideally a hydration pack that holds at least 3L)

- A 1L water bottle

CLOTHES

Footwear

- A pair of broken-in hiking boots

- A pair of comfortable sneakers for camp (sneakers, crocs, etc.)

- Gaiters (optional)

- 3+ pairs of sock liners

- 2+ pairs of warm hiking socks

Upper body

- 3 base layers of wool or synthetic material to keep you warm (no cotton) – think long johns and long-sleeved vests : 2 long-sleeved tops and 1 long legging

- 2 sports t-shirts

- Upper middle layer (like a fleece)

- Windbreaker jacket and rain jacket (2 in 1 is even better)

- Down jacket (your outermost layer for the summit)

Lower body

- 5 pairs of sports underwear and 1 pair of thermal underwear for the summit

- 1-2 hiking trousers

- 1 hiking short (optional, for the days in the rainforest)

- Waterproof trousers (must fit over your hiking trousers)

ACCESSORIES

- Sunhat (ideally with a 360-degree brim)

- Warm hat (beanie)

- Polarized sunglasses

- Lightweight gloves or inner gloves

- Snow gloves or mittens

- Adjustable trekking poles

- Head torch (and extra batteries)

- Camera and/or cellphone

- Powerbank or portable solar charger

- Sports watch

- Plug adaptor (for the hotel)

PERSONAL AND MEDICAL ITEMS

- Toilet paper (you must carry your own during the day)

- Toothbrush and toothpaste

- Wet wipes to wash yourself

- A small, quick-drying towel

- Blister plasters or sports tape

- Insect repellent

- Malaria tablets (Tanzania is in a malaria zone)

- Diarrhea tablets (diarrhea can be a symptom of altitude sickness)

- Painkillers (headaches can be a symptom of altitude sickness)

- Sanitary products (the altitude can disrupt your period cycle – better to be prepared)

- Moisturizing cream (for face and hands)

- Lip balm (with a high SPF)

- Sun cream (with a high SPF against both UVA and UVB)

TRAVEL DOCUMENTS

- Passport (check it's up to date)

- Visa

- Yellow fever vaccination certificate (if applicable)

OPTIONAL OBJECTS

- Favorite snacks (these can offer an energy and mental boost)

- Flavor sachets (the purified water can taste odd to some)

- Playing cards or other games

- Journal and pen

- Earplugs

4. Psychological preparation and stress management for the climb

Climbing a mountain of this size is demanding, not only physically but also mentally, and will generate stress, not mainly because of the altitude and lack of oxygen. You need to be prepared to deal with the mental challenges that will arise as you approach the summit. Psychological preparation and stress management are therefore key to success. In this chapter, we'll be talking about determination, self-confidence, mental preparation and a positive attitude.

Determination : Finding your "reason"

Determination is one of the most important character traits for achieving a goal, especially for a challenge as difficult and demanding as climbing Kilimanjaro. For me, the "reason" I wanted to climb Kilimanjaro was simple: I wanted to take on the challenge of climbing Africa's highest mountain, to get out of my comfort zone and discover my limits. I wanted to prove to myself that I was capable of overcoming these obstacles and persevering in the face of adversity.

However, there was also a deeper reason for this. Climbing Kilimanjaro was a symbol not only of determination, but also of perseverance for me. It was a reminder to myself that I can achieve anything if I put my mind and body to the test. It was a personal challenge that helped me to grow and discover myself.

To keep going, you need strong willpower and motivation, especially when the going gets tough. Particularly on the final climb to the summit, when oxygen becomes increasingly scarce, legs get heavier and heavier, and the altitude makes you dizzy. Understand that it won't be easy, but remember **why** you want to reach the summit (your "reason").

Your determination will be strengthened by the fact that you won't be alone on this mountain. You'll be accompanied by a group of people who share the same passion for hiking and have the same goal as you: to reach the summit. This solidarity and camaraderie will help you maintain your determination and keep going even when the going gets tough.

Self-confidence

When you embark on such an adventure, remember that you're going to face physical and mental challenges you may never have encountered before. It's easy to get discouraged by these difficulties, but if you have confidence in yourself and your abilities, you'll be much more likely to overcome these obstacles.

Listen to your body and trust it. If you're embarking on this adventure, it's because your mind thinks you can do it!

Having self-confidence will also enable you to accept what's happening to you, whether it's stress, fatigue or headaches. If you have confidence in yourself and in your ability to succeed, it will be easier to manage these symptoms and keep moving forward.

Bear in mind that it's perfectly normal to have doubts. When we embarked on this adventure, we didn't know if we'd make it to the top, so we were a little stressed. However, don't let your emotions overwhelm you and enjoy the moment, because the adventure is incredible. Every day you'll be amazed by the beauty of the landscape, whether you're looking at Kilimanjaro or meeting the incredibly friendly local population.

Mental preparation

There are several stages in the mental preparation for such an event.

-   Set yourself achievable goals : It's important to set achievable goals by focusing on the next steps rather than the final destination. For example, think about the next camp rather than the summit, or think about lunch rather than the 8-hour hike (yes, I'm greedy!).

- <u>Manage your expectations</u> : Bear in mind that the climb will be difficult, and don't have unrealistic expectations. Your body will be going through an unprecedented experience, so it's difficult to predict how it will react.

- <u>Prepare for failure</u> : Even if you set out with the intention of succeeding, failure remains a possibility. But that doesn't mean you've failed as a person. Failure should be seen as an opportunity for learning and personal development.

- <u>Practice stress management techniques</u> : There are various techniques you can use to manage stress, such as deep breathing, meditation or regular physical exercise before departure.

- <u>Communicate with your team members</u> : It's important to communicate with your team members and guide about any concerns you may have. Your guide will be able to give you tips and tricks for dealing with stress or mountain sickness. Don't forget that they are there to help you, with the main aim of getting you to the summit in good health.

- <u>Visualisez votre réussite</u> : Taking the time to visualize the stages of your successful climb will help you focus on your goals and feel more confident in your ability to succeed. When you've just reached the top of a big climb, don't hesitate to look back and see how far you've come.

- <u>Prepare your mind for discomfort</u> : We can't stress this enough: climbing Mount Kilimanjaro is a physical challenge, but it's also a mental one, and it's important to prepare for it by getting it into your head that there will be moments of discomfort and pain, but that won't last forever.

- <u>Enjoy every moment</u> : The most important thing is to enjoy every moment, even the difficult ones, because you'll be proud of them! And above all, don't forget to take photos or videos and keep a diary to remind you of everything you've achieved.

Tip:
Really think about taking videos. Photos are good memories, but the brain quickly forgets the sensations. It's harder to relive emotions with photos, but when you watch a video of yourself climbing Kilimanjaro, the feelings come flooding back, allowing you to relive those incredible moments. We took videos throughout the climb with the aim of putting them all together and making a longer video accompanied by music. It's a great souvenir, and has

enabled us to share this extraordinary experience with our family and friends.

A positive attitude - PMA

According to Tanzanians, we need to apply a "PMA", which stands for Positive Mindset Attitude. It's a positive, optimistic mindset that focuses on the positive aspects of life, and sees challenges as opportunities rather than obstacles. PMA is often associated with greater self-confidence and a better ability to deal with stress and uncertainty. Having a PMA will be particularly important for a climb like Kilimanjaro, where the physical and mental challenges will be numerous. PMA is a state of mind, something you can work on and improve over time. For example, instead of thinking about what you still have to do, think about what you've already achieved. Or, instead of thinking about the people you miss, enjoy the company of the local people around you who want to make your experience unforgettable.

To sum up, psychological preparation and stress management are the keys to a successful Kilimanjaro climb. You need to set achievable goals, find your "why", manage expectations, communicate with your team members, but also enjoy every moment. By preparing properly and staying positive, you'll be able to succeed in this incredible adventure and enjoy all it has to offer.

Don't forget that it's normal to have slumps, drops in motivation or moments of doubt about your ability to reach the end. It happens to everyone, and you need to talk about it so that the people around you can reassure and encourage you. If there are several of you in this situation, you can always rely on your guides, who will be there to support you, make you smile and motivate you to keep going. This was the case for me during the night hike to the summit. The effects of altitude were beginning to take their toll on my body and I felt dizzy for much of the walk. Fortunately, my guide encouraged me not to stop until I reached the summit. Similarly, our friend encountered many difficulties and considered giving up on several occasions, but our friendship and cohesion motivated him to keep going. We adapted our pace so that he could keep up with us, and gave him plenty of encouragement, which finally enabled him to reach the summit!

Hakuna Matata!

It's a Swahili expression meaning no problem or no worries! These words perfectly describe the attitude you need to have. Don't worry, let yourself be guided by the experience and good humor of your guides. You're in for an unforgettable vacation that will stay with you forever.

Tanzania is a country full of happiness that is only too happy to share it with its visitors.

5. Choosing a reliable travel agency and calculating your budget

Although I'm not normally a big fan of travel agencies, usually preferring to go on adventures with my backpack and go with the flow, in Kilimanjaro it makes more sense to use them. An experienced travel agency has the expertise to plan your trip in complete safety. The professional guides and porters they hire are trained and experienced in mountain climbing, which is crucial to guaranteeing your safety.

What's more, travel agencies offer complete packages including meals, accommodation (day of arrival/departure, as well as the equipment needed for the climb, such as a tent), climbing permits and transfers, making it much easier to plan your trip. Of course, it's much less stressful to leave the logistical details to someone else, so you can concentrate on the climb itself.

The success of your adventure will therefore depend to some extent on the travel agency you select to accompany you. Choosing a reliable agency is essential, as they work with guides who will ensure your safety and well-being during your ascent of Mount Kilimanjaro. You should therefore find out about their reputation and experience before making your choice. You can, for example, ask for references from other hikers who have already made the ascent, or consult online reviews or blogs.

The KPAP

When choosing an agency, I'd also advise you to make sure it complies with the conditions set by the **KPAP.** The Kilimanjaro Porters Assistance Project (KPAP) is a non-profit organization whose aim is to promote good practice in the treatment of porters on Kilimanjaro. Porters are people employed to carry the equipment and luggage of hikers during their ascent.

KPAP's mission is to improve the working conditions and wages of porters, and to promote their safety and well-being. During my ascent, I noticed that some porters from other agencies were wearing shoes unsuitable for mountain trekking, such as crocs, converse, or victoria shoes with a very thin sole. These shoes are not designed for the harsh conditions of the mountains, and the porters run the risk of injury as they have to walk quickly to get to camp before the hikers. KPAP therefore strives to raise hikers' awareness of the importance of choosing a travel agency that respects ethical standards and good practices in the treatment of porters.

They work really hard to make our trip exceptional and it pained me to see them walking around in bad shoes and without the necessary equipment to stay safe.

To be part of this project, agencies must meet the following conditions:

- Respect the minimum wage for porters agreed by the Kilimanjaro government and stakeholders.
- Pay wages within two days of the descent of an ascent, in accordance with KINAPA regulations.
- Implement a transparent tipping procedure to ensure that porters receive the full amount intended for them.
- Ensure that loads carried by the porter do not exceed 20 kg (excluding the porter's personal belongings).
- Provide porters with three meals a day, of an adequate portion.
- Ensure that porters have adequate shelter and sleeping equipment.
- Ensure that porters are equipped with appropriate hiking gear (shoes, jackets, etc.).
- Take care of sick or injured porters.

If the price quoted for climbing Kilimanjaro seems very low compared to other agencies, it's probably because the organization doesn't respect the points listed above. It's important to understand that the price is generally made up of several elements:

- Transfers from hotel to park entrance and from park exit to hotel.
- Park entrance fees - the price depends on the number of days you spend in the park and is paid directly to the national park administration. For a 7-day trip, the fee is almost 1,000 euros per person. Details of the fees can be found at www.tanzaniaparks.go.tz.
- Minimum wage for the team accompanying you.
- Equipment: tent, comforter, sleeping mat, private toilet, dining tent.
- Meals: breakfast, lunch, snack and dinner.

It's worth pointing out that park entrance fees are fixed, non-negotiable amounts. Moreover, the agencies aim to enable us, as hikers and above all their customers, to reach the summit. To do this, it's essential to be well-equipped for a comfortable night's sleep, and to enjoy well-balanced meals. Generally speaking, agencies try not to neglect these elements to optimize our chances of success. The only element on which agencies can have an impact to reduce their costs is the wages of the local staff present during the climb. But it's thanks to the staff that you can enjoy this incredible experience. They make you feel good, they carry your belongings, they cook for you, they really take care of you.

For popular tours lasting five to seven days, an all-inclusive package generally costs between 1,600 and 2,500 euros per person (excluding flights). The price varies according to the route chosen, the duration and the services and features offered by each agency. If an agency offers a price below this, you can deduce that the climb will not be carried out in the best conditions, and that the team accompanying you will receive a low salary. This will have a direct impact on their family's standard of living and their ability to equip themselves properly.

Compliance with the conditions imposed by KPAP is therefore very important for the well-being of the locals. I strongly recommend that you check whether the travel agency is an approved partner company, certified and verified to meet the standards of porter treatment and safety on the mountain. So, as a trekker, you can be sure that your expedition will be organized responsibly, and that you'll be helping to improve the living conditions of local workers.

Your safety and well-being

Although accessible to anyone in good physical condition, climbing Kilimanjaro is difficult and can be dangerous. Choosing a responsible agency to organize your trip therefore also ensures your safety. They employ experienced people who know the route, the dangers of altitude, the hazards of weather conditions and so on.

From my point of view, I believe that responsible travel operators who treat their carriers fairly are also more likely to offer you, the customer, higher standards of quality, and that carriers who are treated fairly by their companies are also more likely to take your interests into account. First and foremost, this means your security, then your success at the top.

What's more, you depend on your porters to ensure that your water and food are treated properly. In the worst-case scenario, you may have to rely on them for a safe descent. Will your porters be able to do a good job if they're starving, freezing to death and paid considerably less than their colleagues camping right next to your group?

While there are no guarantees, I think booking your climb with a responsible tour operator that treats its employees fairly will be the safer, more ethical choice. Also, it's important to know that any group of trekkers must always be accompanied by an official TANAPA guide. To become a "Lead Guide" or "Assistant Guide", they must undergo appropriate training.

Choosing an agency

Choosing an agency to climb Kilimanjaro is a very personal decision. Some people rely solely on the comments and opinions of others who have made the climb, while others prefer to conduct their own research.

In my case, I was in the first situation. One of my partner's colleagues told him about the incredible experience she'd had during her climb. The feedback on the organization and the people who accompanied her was so positive that we didn't hesitate for a second to choose the same agency for our own ascent.

Of course, we asked whether the agency met the KPAP criteria, and we asked about the itineraries offered, the availability of the desired itinerary and its cost. However, I think it's important to point out that when you embark on a trip of this kind, you shouldn't let the price influence your decision for the reasons given above. It's a unique experience, so if you decide to go for it, choose the agency with whom you have a good feeling, who has a good reputation, even if the cost is 500 euros higher. This is just my point of view, but personally I'd rather pay 500 euros more to have unforgettable memories than save 500 euros and not be completely satisfied with my trip, which will still have cost a few thousand euros.

When it comes to choosing an agency from among all the options available on the market, it's best to do your research according to your personal criteria. There are a number of highly rated agencies, such as Climbing Kilimanjaro, Peak

Planet, Almighty Kilimanjaro, Spider Tours and Safaris, and many others.

I have no experience with these agencies, so it would be inappropriate to speak of their competence and the quality of their excursions. However, I can tell you about my experience with the agency we chose: Follow Alice.

Follow Alice - My experience

Follow Alice was born on Mount Kilimanjaro. While traveling to the roof of Africa, Swiss childhood friends Reto and Daniel met Chris from Tanzania. After their climb, the three of them came up with a bold and exciting plan: to build a modern, sustainably-run travel company by travelers, for travelers.

Today, in addition to climbing Kilimanjaro, Follow Alice offers other adventures for small or large groups, including a trek to see rare gorillas in Uganda's dense jungle and a trek across the mighty Himalayas to reach Everest base camp.

The aim of this travel agency is to comply with the principles of responsible tourism. To guide their decisions, they take care to respect four axes: offering employment opportunities for local entrepreneurs, benefiting the local community and economy, protecting the wildlife visited and not harming the environment visited.

As explained above, it was very important for us to choose an agency committed to respecting not only the country and its nature, but also the locals through compliance with the conditions imposed by KPAP.

What's more, it's interesting to know that each tour is managed by a dedicated travel manager and an experienced local Follow Alice leader on site. Given the agency's human scale, our experience was seamless and highly personalized. We were in regular contact with our travel manager for any additional questions we had. Which is great when you're about to embark on a trip where preparation is crucial.
Once in Tanzania, our point of contact was local leader Chris, who organizes every trip using local people. He has an exceptional background and his long personal experience makes him a person we can trust. He started out as a porter in 1999, then became Lead Guide, and finally joined Follow Alice as local leader. He has climbed Kilimanjaro over 300 times! Who could be better than Chris to organize your Kilimanjaro climb?

Talking to the inhabitants of Moshi (one of the departure towns), we found that many of them had worked at least once as porters accompanying tourists on their Kilimanjaro ascents with various travel agencies. Not all of them have continued because of the poor working conditions sometimes put in place by the agencies, but we can see that it's an activity that sustains several villages around the mountain. Without our climbs, many of them would not have had jobs. So we were delighted to be accompanied by local people on this new adventure.

We decided to carry out this experience during our summer vacation in July 2022, and as mentioned in the first chapter, we opted for the seven-day Lemosho route. Our group consisted of four people: an Italian woman we didn't know, my partner, a friend and myself. If you're traveling in a group, it's also possible to book for a larger number of people by indicating the total number when booking with your travel manager. If you prefer to climb Kilimanjaro on your own, it depends on the travel agency, but is usually possible at a higher rate. Personally, I enjoyed doing the climb with someone I didn't know, as it enabled us to meet someone who shared our love of travel and with whom we kept in touch. It really added something to our experience.

For our group of four hikers, no fewer than twenty locals accompanied us on the climb. That's 5 locals per hiker! These twenty people included:
- A lead guide
- An assistant guide
- A chef
- Seventeen porters, including four porters with additional responsibilities (waiter, tent erector, sous-chef and toilet attendant).

This number of companions is the minimum required if the agency wishes to comply with KPAP conditions. I remind you that each team member may carry no more than 20 kilograms, and that the total weight of the equipment must be evenly distributed, without exceeding this imposed limit.

On the day of departure, Follow Alice picked us up from our lodge and drove us to the entrance of the national park. During the hour-long minibus journey, we had the opportunity to meet the entire team and discuss the day's program with our main guide. As soon as we arrived, we noticed that the guides were all very attentive to our needs and did everything to ensure our well-being and our progress to the summit.

As explained in Chapter 2, diet is a crucial element in a successful sporting challenge. And we were pleasantly surprised by the meals prepared by the chef and his sous-chef throughout our climb. Every day, we had complete, balanced and, above all, delicious meals! The menu was carefully put together to provide us with all the nutrients we needed to reach the summit.

In addition to the good food, we also noticed that Follow Alice has quality safety procedures in place. At the end of each day, we were monitored with a pulse oximeter. This measures the oxygen saturation in your blood, which helps to understand how someone copes with altitude. In this way, our guide could assess whether we were in good shape to continue our ascent at altitude.

Looking back on our ascent, I'm really glad I chose this travel agency, as I have no negative feedback to offer. Whether in terms of communication, preparation, organization, logistics or meals, everything was of the highest quality. I hope you'll have the same experience as I did, and that you'll treasure your memories!

The budget

As mentioned earlier, although budget shouldn't be your main concern, it's understandable that you'd like to have a rough idea of how much this adventure will cost. And it certainly won't be cheap.

Bear in mind that it's difficult to determine a precise budget for every situation, as it depends on a number of factors. These include:
-   Travel from your place of residence to Tanzania
-   Travel documents (visa, passport if you don't have one)
-   The ascent
-   The tips you'll give
-   The equipment you have to purchase.

Transportation costs to Tanzania

This first element will depend on your departure location and the time of year you plan to travel. Living in an area without an international airport nearby, we decided to fly out of Barcelona airport. This international airport offered flights at various times with numerous airlines at advantageous prices.

To give you an idea of the costs, here's what I paid for the flights, adding a stopover in Zanzibar:
Barcelona to Kilimanjaro: 905.00 euros
Kilimanjaro to Zanzibar: 124.00 euros
Zanzibar to Barcelona: 791.00 euros.

The total for my trip including Zanzibar is **1,820 euros**. However, if you decide not to go via Zanzibar, it's likely that you can get a return flight at a more attractive rate. Also, our trip took place in the middle of summer, from July 16 to August 6, so it's possible to pay a little less if you travel outside the summer season.

Travel documents

To travel to Tanzania, you need a valid passport (at least 6 months) and a visa. As mentioned, the visa can be obtained online or on arrival in Tanzania, but it is advisable to apply online before departure to avoid long waits at the airport. The current cost of a tourist visa for Tanzania is $50, or around **47 euros**. This rate may change over time.

In addition, if you are arriving in Tanzania from (or transiting through) a country where yellow fever is endemic, you will also need to present a yellow fever vaccination certificate. The countries concerned may vary, so it is advisable to check the latest information with an international vaccination center or the Tanzanian embassy in your country.

Travelers should also ensure they have adequate travel insurance to cover any health problems, trip cancellation or loss of luggage. It is advisable to consult the travel recommendations issued by government authorities to get an idea of the latest requirements and safety information in force for Tanzania. As previously mentioned, I opted for True Traveller, taking the Traveller Plus Policy (Area 4) and the Adventure Pack Add-on which includes Kilimanjaro. Please note that you must have +5000m insurance to climb Kilimanjaro. For a 23-day trip, this cost me **120 euros**.

The climb

The cost of climbing Kilimanjaro can vary considerably depending on many factors, such as duration, the level of comfort you're looking for, the number of people in your group, the travel agency you book with and more. In general, costs range from 1,600 to 4,000 euros per person.

Travel agencies offer all-inclusive packages that generally include permits, meals, accommodation, some equipment, guides and porters, as well as transfers to and from the airport. Costs may seem high, but remember that climbing Kilimanjaro is a challenging and expensive adventure that requires careful planning and professional assistance to ensure the safety and comfort of hikers. Also bear in mind that during the 7-day ascent, you won't have any other expenses, compared to a traditional vacation where we're constantly tempted to spend (restaurants, activities etc.).

As mentioned above, part of the cost of the climb will be paid to the national park administration for entry and camping fees. On top of this, you'll have to pay for food and wages for guides and porters, which are calculated on a daily basis. So, the longer your climb, the more expensive it will be. So it's important to assess which itinerary suits your budget, but be careful not to choose a route that's too short, as this may reduce your chances of success.

Our group had chosen the Lemosho route for seven days, which I thought was perfect to allow our bodies to adapt to the altitude. The first few days of walking were the longest, leaving us time for shorter walks on the final days, to rest in the afternoons and conserve our strength for the final ascent to the summit.

For this route, we had paid around **2,600 euros** per person. This included transport to and from the airport, as well as two nights at the lodge (one night on arrival in Kilimanjaro and one night before departure for Zanzibar).

To facilitate our acclimatization, we decided to take a four-night/five-day safari before starting our Kilimanjaro ascent. If you'd like to do the same, there is an additional cost. To give you an idea, our safari with the same travel agency cost around 2,300 euros. Meals and accommodation are also included in this package.

The tips

Tipping is a widespread social practice in Tanzania, and Kilimanjaro workers are accustomed to receiving tips from hikers at the end of each ascent. These tips form an important part of their income and are tax-exempt for them. Most agencies pay their porters fairly, in line with the guidelines set by the Kilimanjaro Porters Assistance Project (KPAP), but this is not enough to live on. So tips play an important role in rewarding the crew for their hard work.

To regulate and balance the practice of tipping, a ceremony called the "tipping ceremony" has been introduced. It usually takes place on the penultimate day of your ascent, before dinner. Your travel agent should provide you with detailed information on how the ceremony takes place and how much to tip, but in general, it is recommended to tip at least 10% of the cost of the tour. In my case, for example, the Kilimanjaro climb cost around 2,600 euros, so you'd need to tip at least 260 euros. The amount is then divided according to the status of the team members, with the head guide generally receiving a larger share than the porters. The ceremony begins with a Swahili song sung by the team in honor of the Kilimanjaro expedition. Then, one of the hikers in the group takes the floor to announce the amount of tips received by each team member.

In our group of four hikers, we had given $320 per person (around **300 euros**) in tips to the entire crew, making a total of $1,280.

The purchase of your equipment

The cost of the equipment needed to climb Kilimanjaro can vary considerably depending on the quality and quantity of the items you choose, as well as what you already own. Essentials include hiking boots, waterproof and breathable clothing, hiking poles, a backpack, sunglasses, a headlamp, a water bottle, a first-aid kit, a hat and gloves, among others. It's important to invest in quality items to ensure your safety and comfort during the climb. Depending on the items you choose, the cost can vary from a few dozen to hundreds of euros. You can also rent certain items from equipment rental stores or your travel agent if you don't want to buy all the equipment you need.

Below you'll find a list of all the equipment I had to buy to complete the climb, with an indication of cost:

- Millet 40L backpack: 160 euros
- Salewa hiking boots: 200 euros
- North Face waterproof and windproof jacket: 150 euros
- Cimalp fleece jacket: 80 euros
- Four pairs of socks for long-distance hiking and cold weather: 65 euros
- Forclaz hiking pants: 50 euros
- Decathlon rain pants: 10 euros
- Forclaz wool leggings: 40 euros
- 2 Forclaz wool long-sleeve undershirts: 80 euros
- Decathlon under-gloves: 10 euros
- Waterproof Duffle Bag Forclaz : 70 euros
- Decathlon hiking poles: 20 euros
- Stoots headlamp: 128 euros
- Decathlon water pouch and 1-liter bottle: 15 euros
- Decathlon neck cover: 5 euros
- Crocs : 45 euros
- External battery : 40 euros
- Anti-malaria drugs, 3 boxes of 12 tablets : 75 euros

Here is the equipment I rented from my Follow Alice travel agency :

- Down jacket : 40 dollars
- Gloves : 5 dollars

As well as the equipment provided by my travel agency included in the cost of the climb :

- Sleeping tent
- Meal tent
- Down
- Small mattress
- Toilet

And the equipment I already owned :

- Sports T-shirts
- Sunglasses
- Cap
- Hat
- iPhone for photos/videos
- Garmin sports watch
- Sports underwear.

The total cost of my equipment is **1,288 euros**. As mentioned earlier, this amount will vary according to the equipment you buy, its quality and what you already own.

As this was my first ascent of this kind, I had to buy almost everything. However, these purchases won't go to waste, and will come in handy on future adventures.

Having detailed each component, we can see that the final cost of my adventure is composed of :
- Cost of transport to Tanzania (excluding Kilimanjaro-Zanzibar flight): 1,696 euros
- Travel documents (Visa+Insurance): 167 euros
- Climbing: 2,600 euros
- Tips: 300 euros
- Equipment purchase: 1,288 euros

For my Kilimanjaro climb, the total cost came to **6,051 euros**. This is a considerable amount, which is why it's important to point out that the cost of this type of trip is not limited to simply booking with an agency. Other expenses, such as plane tickets, insurance and equipment, are added to this amount, more than doubling the final cost. Before embarking on such an adventure, make sure you have the necessary funds to complete the trip with complete peace of mind.

To sum up, choosing a reliable travel agency is a key element in guaranteeing a successful trip to Kilimanjaro. By taking the time to do your research, read the reviews of previous clients and ask questions to ensure that the agency meets your needs and expectations, you can be sure of finding a reliable, serious and competent agency. The budget required for such an expedition can vary considerably, depending on the choice of agency, equipment, tips and other factors. Plan a realistic budget, taking all these factors into account. However, even if the amount may seem high, the experience you'll have will be one of a kind and will leave you with unforgettable memories. So save some money and go for it!

6. Preparing your hiking gear and organizing your backpack

Preparing your hiking gear and backpack is essential for a successful Kilimanjaro ascent. You need to be prepared for the changing weather conditions, extreme temperatures and physical challenges you'll encounter. Also make sure you distribute the weight evenly in your backpack, to avoid unnecessary burden and making your climb more difficult. Here are a few key points to consider when preparing.

Preparing your equipment

As you've probably already realized, the most important piece of equipment you'll need is your hiking boots. This is the only thing that's difficult, if not impossible, to rent locally, as every foot is different. During your ascent, many kilometers will be covered, so it's more than important to be comfortable in your shoes. If they're new, we recommend that you walk at least 100 kilometers in them before climbing Kilimanjaro.

Here's a little tip: if possible, pack your shoes in your hand luggage and take them with you in the cabin (in your backpack, for example). This way, if your checked luggage is lost or delayed, you'll still be able to start your ascent. In fact, almost all equipment can be rented on site, with the exception of shoes. So make sure you don't lose them!

In addition to your shoes, it's also a good idea to train with your backpack. In this way, you'll get used to having a weight on your back, be able to assess whether it's too heavy, position the straps correctly, and so on. It's important to hike with your backpack when you're training, because if you're not used to it, your back, shoulders and neck can quickly become sore.

If, like me, your 3L water pouch is brand new, I'd advise you to rinse it well before use to remove the plastic taste. To do this, fill the water pouch and squeeze out the water. Repeat until the plastic taste has disappeared.

It's also worth checking your external battery. Charge it fully and check the number of charges possible. That way, you'll know how many times you can charge your device and save battery power if necessary. It would be a shame to run out of battery power to record a video of your arrival at the summit!

As for all the garments, you can also test them during your training sessions to see how comfortable you feel in them. However, it's difficult to test everything unless you're in climatic conditions similar to those you'll encounter on your climb.

Organizing your backpack (the one you will carry yourself)

We're talking here about your backpack, which you'll take with you on your day's walk. The volume of this bag will be limited to a maximum of 45L, so you'll need to take only the essentials with you.

First of all, it's vital to choose the right clothing for the day's hiking ahead. For example, on the first day of your hike, which generally takes place in the forest, the weather can be hot, heavy or humid, depending on the season. Light clothing is therefore recommended, as humidity and heat can quickly raise your body temperature. On the other hand, temperatures at altitude will drop considerably, especially on the third and fourth days. You'll need warm clothing to protect you from the cold and wind. For these days, you'll need your fleece, windproof jacket and even a hat.

It's a good idea to ask your guide for advice on what clothes to bring, depending on the expected weather conditions. Bear in mind, however, that during the day, you'll only be able to take your 45L backpack with you, so it's important to choose the clothes you really need and leave the rest of your belongings with the porters. You'll only find them at the end of the day at camp.

Altitude will have unexpected effects on your body, so you need to be prepared for this. For example, you may experience headaches, nausea or dizziness. So it's a good idea to bring a first-aid kit with you, containing medicines that can relieve these symptoms.

In addition to the physical effects of altitude, long walks and fatigue, your mind can also be affected. That's why I advise you to bring along your favorite snacks, which will boost you when you encounter any difficulties.

Then there are a few things you should always have in your bag, such as sunglasses, sun cream, SPF50 lip balm, cap, camera or telephone, walking sticks, toilet paper, rubbish bag and all your personal documents and wallet.

To complete the above items, you will of course have your water bag, which the team will fill every morning and, if necessary, during the day. Usually, there's a specially-designed pocket in your backpack to hang your water bag and pass the tube through, but this depends on the brand.

To sum up, here's a list of things to pack in your rucksack for the day's hike, depending of course on the weather forecast for your week's travel:
-   Rain gear: pants, jacket/poncho

- Warm clothing: fleece, windproof jacket, gloves, hat. Depending on the weather, you may also need a down jacket before the summit.
- Sun protection: cap, sunglasses, sunscreen, SPF50 lip balm.
- Snacks (sweet or salty)
- Three liters of water
- Walking sticks
- Camera and/or cell phone
- Small emergency pharmacy (plasters, compeed for blisters, painkillers, diarrhea tablets, personal medicines, etc.). If you're a woman, don't forget your sanitary products, as altitude can sometimes trigger menstruation.
- Wallet and personal documents
- Toilet paper
- Ecological, compostable garbage bag for all your garbage.

7. Tips for acclimating to oxygen deprivation and altitude

The biggest challenge in climbing Mount Kilimanjaro is acclimating to the lack of oxygen at altitude. It's possible to prepare yourself a little with training, but it's impossible to predict how your body will react when you're on Africa's highest mountain. So, to help your body adapt as much as possible, I've listed a few tips that will help you prepare for the climb.

Take your time

The first tip for acclimating to altitude and oxygen deprivation is to plan a gradual ascent. I strongly advise against rushing to altitude, as this can lead to altitude sickness (headache, dizziness, vomiting).

It is therefore advisable to plan intermediate stages to allow the body to adapt to the low atmospheric pressure and lack of oxygen. This is why the Kilimanjaro ascent offers several itineraries ranging from five to nine days, or even longer. If you choose a five-day route, you run the risk of your body not acclimating properly to the lack of oxygen, and of having to descend without reaching the summit. It is therefore generally advisable to choose a fairly long itinerary to allow your body to acclimate gradually and thus increase your chances of success. That's why I myself chose a seven-day itinerary, which represents a good average between the shortest and longest routes.

If you're an experienced hiker, you may be tempted to pick up your pace and push your body, but this can be counterproductive. On the contrary, you need to concentrate on your breathing and regulate your heart rate according to the physical effort you're putting in. To keep your pace slow, you can rely on your guides. They will regularly remind you that the key to success is to go "pole pole" (which means slowly in Swahili).

Stay hydrated

Drinking plenty of water is essential for altitude acclimatization. At high altitudes, the air is drier and the body loses more water through breathing. So it's vital to drink enough water to compensate for this loss and avoid dehydration and headaches.

The World Health Organization (WHO) recommends drinking at least 3 liters of water a day at altitude. This may sound like a lot, but it's essential to maintain good hydration and promote acclimatization.

In addition to water, I also can recommend drinking electrolyte-rich beverages. These drinks help maintain the body's water and electrolyte balance, which is crucial for acclimatization. You can buy sachets or tablets to mix with water; simply put a tablet in your water bag to enjoy its benefits. This will also add a slight taste to your water that's not unpleasant!

When it comes to hydration too, you can rely on your guides. They'll regularly remind you to "sippy sippy".

Avoid alcohol and sleeping pills

When acclimating to altitude, it's best to avoid alcohol and sleeping pills. Alcohol has a negative impact on acclimatization, increasing the effects of altitude sickness, such as headaches, nausea and dizziness. What's more, alcohol dehydrates the body, aggravating altitude symptoms.

Similarly, sleeping pills can disrupt sleep and reduce the body's ability to acclimatize to altitude. Sleep is crucial for acclimatization, as it is during sleep that the body recovers and prepares itself for the physical effort ahead. Sleeping pills disrupt this important recovery phase.

Eat properly

Proper nutrition is essential for acclimatization. It's important to eat balanced, nutritious meals that provide sufficient calories and nutrients to sustain the intense physical effort of hiking at altitude. Meals should also be easy to digest to avoid stomach upset and nausea.

Carbohydrate-rich foods such as pasta, rice, bread and fruit are recommended to provide your body with energy. Proteins are also important to help rebuild muscles damaged by the physical efforts. Fresh fruit and vegetables are of course recommended for their high vitamin and mineral content. Don't worry, the chef will prepare complete meals for you throughout your ascent.

As altitude increases, appetite is likely to decrease. It is therefore advisable to eat more when you still have an appetite. So make the most of every breakfast, lunch and dinner to fill up on nutrients and contribute to muscle recovery and regeneration. All you have to do is get your feet under the table and enjoy a delicious meal cooked by the chef!

The symptoms of altitude sickness, such as nausea and vomiting, can affect appetite, but it's essential to keep eating and drinking enough to maintain good hydration and energy. Trust your guides and discuss your symptoms with them so they can give you advice on what to do. To give you an example, at the end of the second day, my partner experienced headaches, stomach aches and nausea that affected his appetite. The guide advised him to force himself to eat and, above all, to drink hot water with lime juice. The latter had a direct impact on his nausea and he felt much better!

Breathe deeply

The lack of oxygen at high altitude can lead to rapid, shallow breathing. To avoid this, it's important to breathe deeply and evenly. Take deep, slow breaths to oxygenate your body and avoid dizziness or discomfort.

It's also a good idea to concentrate on the exhalation phase, as this is when the body eliminates carbon dioxide, a waste product that accumulates more rapidly at high altitude. Try to prolong your exhalation to help your body get rid of this carbon dioxide and better regulate your breathing rhythm.

Finally, it's a good idea to practice diaphragmatic breathing, which allows you to breathe more deeply and efficiently. To do this, inhale by inflating your belly rather than your chest, then exhale slowly by drawing in your belly. This can help oxygenate your body more effectively and maintain a regular breathing rhythm.

Prepare medication in case of need

If you experience headaches, stomach aches or nausea, you can take medication to relieve the symptoms. These are available over the counter in pharmacies (paracetamol, doliprane, advil). The same applies to Imodium. The name of each medication can vary depending on your country of residence.

A consultation with your doctor is essential if you wish to obtain medication to facilitate acclimatization, such as acetazolamide (diamox). This medication can help reduce the symptoms of altitude sickness, but should not be used as a substitute for gradual acclimation. Your doctor's advice is essential to determine whether this medication is suitable for your medical condition and to establish an appropriate adjustment plan. If you decide to take this type of medication, be sure to inform your guide.

Acclimate before departure

The best way to get your body used to altitude is to go up regularly. If you live in a mountainous region, you're in luck, so make the most of it. When you go on training hikes, don't hesitate to choose routes at increasingly higher altitudes. Being active during these climbs will allow your body to adapt and improve your breathing. If you live in a fairly flat area like I do, you can plan weekends in the mountains to do two consecutive days of hiking. We also chose to do a safari before climbing Kilimanjaro, as the national parks are at a higher altitude than where we live. Please note that many people choose to do the safari after the ascent, so this is also an option. However, for reasons of acclimation, it seemed us wiser to do it before the ascent.

It's important to understand that even the best athletes can't predict altitude sickness. Just because you've never had it doesn't mean you won't get it on Kilimanjaro. You just have to accept it!

In conclusion, altitude acclimation is an important process to consider when making a high-altitude ascent. Following the rules of slow progress, staying well hydrated and eating properly are essential to allow the body to gradually adapt to changes in atmospheric pressure and oxygen deprivation. Finally, breathing properly and taking medication if necessary can help reduce the risk of acute mountain sickness and increase the chances of a successful ascent. By following these tips, you can prepare your body to cope with altitude and make the most of your Kilimanjaro experience.

8. Tips for dealing with health and safety issues during the climb

Climbing Kilimanjaro is an adventure to be taken seriously, as it involves risks to the health and safety of hikers. For this reason, it is important to take into account the following advice:

Listen to your body

Watch out for altitude-related symptoms such as headaches, nausea, fatigue and dizziness. If you experience them, don't ignore them. Inform your guide or assistant guide immediately and follow their advice.

It's important to understand that everyone reacts differently to altitude and low oxygen pressure, so even if you're in good health and physical condition, you may still experience altitude symptoms. Listening to your body and reacting accordingly is essential to ensure your safety during the climb.

Respect safety rules

Follow the safety rules laid down by your guide. Don't take unnecessary risks or stray from the group without authorization.

Stay hydrated

I can't repeat this enough: it's vital to drink enough water to avoid dehydration, which can aggravate altitude-related symptoms. To stay hydrated, you need to drink regularly throughout the day, even if you're not thirsty. It's advisable to drink around 3 to 4 liters of water a day at altitude. Forcing yourself to drink will only benefit you! It's one of the keys to success.

Use appropriate equipment

The use of appropriate equipment is essential to ensure your safety and comfort during the climb. The most important thing is to wear sturdy, comfortable hiking boots suitable for mountain walking. They must offer good grip on rocky and slippery surfaces, as well as good support for the ankles to prevent the risk of slipping, falling or injury. By choosing the right footwear, you can continue your hike without pain or risk of injury.

Follow medical protocols

If you are taking medication, make sure you have enough for the duration of the climb. If you have any known medical conditions, be sure to let your guide know before you go.

As mentioned, you must have a first aid kit on hand at all times. Headaches or nausea can occur at any time of the day, so it is crucial to have the necessary medications to ensure peace of mind while walking.

In conclusion, it is essential to maintain good physical health while climbing Mount Kilimanjaro. Make sure you have basic medications and know how to manage common health problems such as diarrhea and headaches. It is important to inform your guide as soon as the first symptoms of mountain sickness appear so that he can give you appropriate advice. Also, thanks to their experience, the guides are able to reduce risks in the mountains and know how to react to guarantee your safety. Above all, don't worry, everything will be fine. Personally, I had a little headache during the fifth and sixth day and it was largely bearable. Hakuna matata, you will make it!

9. Tips for respecting the environment and Mount Kilimanjaro's ecosystem

Climbing this wonderful mountain is an incredible experience, but we must do it responsibly. Mount Kilimanjaro is a fragile and vulnerable ecosystem. Although it is not currently considered to be in immediate danger, it faces many environmental challenges such as climate change, land degradation and pollution. Global warming is of particular concern because it has direct consequences on the melting of Kilimanjaro's glaciers, which are a vital source of water for local populations. The loss of ice could also have an impact on local biodiversity and the stability of the ecosystem in general. It is therefore crucial to continue monitoring the condition of Mount Kilimanjaro and take steps to protect and preserve it for future generations. Here are some tips to respect the mountain during your ascent :

Respect the rules of the national park

To protect the environment, park authorities have implemented strict regulations. It is imperative to respect these rules, in particular by not leaving any waste on the mountain and avoiding disturbing the fauna and flora. It is also prohibited to bring plastic bags on the mountain and encouraged to use ecological and compostable trash bags to dispose of your waste.

Use the toilets provided to you

Dry toilets are available along the way, but their number is limited and they are often very dirty. It is best to take advantage of the toilets provided by your travel agency at the camps (morning and evening). If you have to relieve yourself during the day in the great outdoors, it is important to put your used toilet paper in a trash bag. So make sure you always have a biodegradable trash bag and a roll of toilet paper with you.

Avoid disposable products

Disposable products, such as plastic water bottles, are very polluting. Opt for reusable products, such as a stainless steel water bottle, to avoid generating unnecessary waste. If you have snacks wrapped in plastic, make sure to put them in your trash bag once you're done eating them so you don't leave trash on the mountain.

Respect the fauna and flora

It is important to stay on marked trails to avoid trampling vegetation and disturbing wildlife. It is also essential to avoid feeding animals, picking flowers or plants, and preserving natural habitats.

By following these simple tips, you can help preserve Mount Kilimanjaro's unique environment for future generations.

"A journey of a thousand miles begins with a single step."

Lao-Tseu

Conclusion

So, do you feel ready? I hope you are motivated!

You now know the mountain, its different hiking routes and should probably already have an idea of the route you are going to choose. You can now work on your physical condition by following the advice in the booklet while going at your own pace. Even more exciting, you can start choosing your agency, booking your trip as well as listing the necessary equipment and everything else you still need to purchase.

As explained in the booklet, it is completely normal to feel stressed for such an adventure, it remains a challenge. Don't worry, it will be a good stress that will motivate you to surpass yourself because I repeat again, everyone can reach the top. Stay positive, believe in yourself and enjoy what Tanzania has to offer!

And Tanzania has a lot to offer. I highly recommend you consider going on a safari if you've never done one. Several lengths of stay are offered ranging from 3 to 5 days (sometimes even more). Our 5-day safari allowed us to cover a large area of the various national parks and see all the animals living there. They call me an 'animal lover' so you can imagine how happy I was to see lions, giraffes, elephants, hyenas, leopards, cheetahs and many other animals in their natural habitat. I promise you, a zoo is nothing compared with what you'll experience here... Let yourself be tempted, you only live once!

WARNINGS

The information contained in this booklet is given for educational purposes. The reader must deepen them through their own research and adapt their trip according to their own desires and needs.

Made in the USA
Monee, IL
24 December 2024

75338087R00069